BEHIND THE BUSH

"INTIMACY WITH GOD"

EJF PUBLISHING HOUSE

CHICAGO, ILLINOIS

Copyright © 2022 by Nicole Trent

All rights reserved. No part of this publication may be reproduced, distributed, or transmitted in any form or by any means, without prior written permission.

Nicole Trent/EJF Publishing House Publisher's Note: This is a work of nonfiction. Names, characters, places, and incidents are a product of the author's imagination.

Locales and public names are sometimes used for atmospheric purposes. Any resemblance to actual people, living or dead, or to businesses, companies, events, institutions, or locales is completely coincidental.

Behind The Burning Bush "Intimacy with God.
-- 1st ed. ISBN 978-1-7368985-4-3

Dedication

To my darling husband and children, thank you for believing in me! You all have had patience with me, as I took time to write what was in my heart. Love you all dearly.

I dedicate this book to individuals and families who are yearning to know what's behind the burning bush. May you find your intimate place in God.

Prophetess Nicole Trent

CONTENTS

Introduction 1

Chapter 1: Spousal Prayer 11

Chapter 2: Developing A Prayer A Life 23

Chapter 3: Born Again 29

Chapter 4: Unselfish Prayer 37

Chapter 5: Patience 51

Chapter 6: 2 Chronicles 7:14 63

Chapter 7: Hear from Heaven 73

INTRODUCTION

Behind The Bush "Intimacy With God"

I would like you to remember that according to the book of Romans 10:17 that faith cometh by hearing, and hearing by the Word of God. So, I know we hear a lot of cliches from people and allow the Scripture people use to speak those things that are not as they already are, name it to claim it, walk into your blessing, and so forth. Beloved, the reality is hearing what God has said or spoken over your life. That is what you will have to be accounted for. The activation of your faith is what matters to walking into what God said He has for you. The Scripture says in Matthew 6:33 NIV, but seek his Kingdom and righteousness first, and all these things will also be given to you. God already has a divine directive for every one of our lives, but it is left for us to choose the path we must follow. In everything in life, we need divine direction. Many have made costly mistakes because they were not privileged to have a divine direction. We noticed that it was because of the sin in the Garden of Eden that brought separation between God and man. We have a will, and then there is God's will. Most of the time, our will super seize the will of God for our life. This happens when we are committed to ourselves instead of God. A situation whereby we have our desires or stubborn will. Some of us want to do what we want with our self-power. As you can see, just like children, we may tell them not to touch the hot stove, but before we know it, they will touch it because of their desire to know why we said they should not touch it.

Sometimes we don't wait for God's will to happen; we expect our own will to happen, which leads us nowhere. We have the purpose of walking in complete fulfillment, but we must align with God's plan for our life. Take what God has given you and do your best for His glory. God can do a lot with a little. Yes, some may develop their path earlier; for example, some knew what they wanted to do from childhood. They knew they wanted to be a preacher, wanted to be a doctor, and wanted to be a teacher.

But, for some, it is not that simple; they have to go through a lot and view the wilderness experience before getting to the path God wants them to be in. If you're facing a big decision, you may wish God would write His will for you on the wall or speak audibly. But He rarely chooses to make His will for your life that obvious. Instead, He wants you to be persistent in seeking His guidance. Ephesians 5:15 GNT says, "So be careful how you live. Don't live like ignorant people, but likewise people."

So, it is good to hear what God is saying, but when it comes to hearing the Word of God, the question is, how shall they hear without a preacher? How can they preach unless they've been sent? This one thing is sure everyone is not sent to preach the

Word of God, but everyone must be under a pastor that can nourish their spiritual growth. This is why we have false prophets arisen. Some have a zeal for the work of God, but they haven't gone through the proper channels to obtain the gifts of God. God speaks to us individually, and He can sometimes speak through assignments, visions, and dreams. He could speak through someone sending you a message. There are different ways that God speaks to us, but I wanted to clarify that you must hear what God is saying to move forward. So, we must be aware of false prophets speaking into our life. Remember, their job is to confuse and derail from your purpose. He is confusing us. Second, we must be careful who is speaking in our ears. So, you see, that faith is fundamental when building our relationship with Him and obtaining the things that God has for us. Also, understand that the Scripture says that if we abide in Him, He will abide in us and that we should ask whatsoever in His name that will be given to us. So yes, we have to hope in God, for He will give us the things we desire as we seek Him. He will give us things we didn't even ask for because He is that faithful. Yes, it is a faith journey, and so faith begets faith, and to go to Jesus, in the first place, requires faith. We, the people of God, have this assurance and this access that the Lord is our Shepherd and that we shall not want. That's got to hold so much weight because when you are a sheep of His, and you are following His instructions, leadership, and directives, there's one thing that we can rest assured of, which is to be confident that we shall not want for any good thing. He shall supply all that we need according to His riches and glory. The only way to obtain access is by hearing the Word of God. Obtain entrance through Salvation and hearing through the man or woman of God preaching to us.

(Examples of hearing)

When I was a little girl, I remember about 8. I was outside in the front yard, and someone called my name. I thought it was my mother, so I went in. "Ma, you called me?" She said no. This happened to me three times. I didn't realize that was the voice of God. Anytime you hear someone, whether in person or a group sharing the gift of Salvation, that's a form of hearing (through evangelistically street meetings, someone passing tracks.) Another example of hearing God's voice is when He told me in 2015 that I would have twins.

Also, know that God will speak a word, and things will begin to manifest. He speaks to cause a dramatic change that should come in your present or near future, whether marriage, moving to a new state, or embarking on a new career path. God will speak and inform you of these things.

Isaiah 55:11, "so is my Word that goes out from my mouth: It will not return to me empty but will accomplish what I desire and achieve the purpose for which I sent it."

There is irresistible supernatural power in God's Word; it will not return to Him empty. God gives us information on a need-to-know basis. We might not get clarity into everything He's telling us, but as time passes, we will understand, and just like a pregnant woman, she knows she's pregnant, but she doesn't know the expected due date; she never really knows when that baby will come. So now that you have something or we have things that have been deposited in our belly, and we know they are due to come forth, let us wait through the process, and the baby is going to be born through faith because faith comes by hearing and hearing the Word of God. So, we must continue as Christians to walk in faith, speak in faith, live in faith, and see faith as an essential thing we have to live on.

Prayer:

Father, in the name of Jesus, I pray that faith will be activated in the lives of Your people as they hear Your Word, God, as they begin to seek Your face and not walk in their understanding but in all our ways to acknowledge You. God, I pray that You will direct our path to believe the Word today. Hallelujah, You're faithful and forgive us for our unrighteousness. After this day, I pray that we will begin to walk in clarity and newness of mind and thought. Let the ear gates be open to hearing You and only You. I bind the spirit of confusion, negativity, and doubt. I bind every satanic device that comes to interfere and stop the Word of God from taking root and bringing forth fruit in the mighty name of Jesus. Thank You, God; in Jesus' name, we pray. Amen.

CHAPTER 1:
SPOUSAL PRAYER

It has been eight years in ministry working alongside my husband, who is a pastor. This subject, to me, is a sensitive, heartfelt emotional topic, and I have found in my years in ministry how crucial it is to pray for your spouse. The enemy, Satan, has attacked the relationships between husband and wife. If he breaks down the relationship, the bond between the husband and wife, and puts a division in between, the children will fall vulnerable to the attack of Satan. Marriages must stay together on one accord and bond to be truly effective. This attack hits all nationalities and cultural backgrounds. We're all fighting the same war; the war against the Devil himself. The woman is essential in praying for her family, especially her husband. If the Devil can attack and afflict the head of the family, it leaves vulnerability to the wife and the children.

I think it's important to remember that we wrestle not against flesh and blood but principalities, powers, the rulers of the darkness of this world, and brutal wickedness in high places (See Ephesians 6 and 12). Husband and wife, when we get upset, we tend to fight with words, and sometimes we say some hurtful things to get a reaction. Men and women don't interact in the same way. Women tend to be more vocal; we like to talk about things, feelings or emotions, but men do the opposite. Men are calm, unlike women. Women read into things…yes, we want details. Men don't finish their sentences, they jump from phrase to phrase, and we must read between the lines. When men get hurt, they don't show it, but when women are hurt, they show their feelings. I have tried the silent treatment, the 'don't touch me,' I tried not fixing his dinner and telling him to wash his clothes. Listen, ladies, none of these things work because men just don't get it ....marriage was never intended for one to be under the control of one person. It was a union of two working together to get things accomplished. This is why it's so important to keep God at the Center. The Devil does not want to see marriages work because God ordains marriage. So, we wrestle not with flesh, our husbands, or our wives, but with the enemy who comes to attack the marriage. I have had lies told about my husband; if it weren't for my relationship with Jesus Christ, I probably would have fallen for it. This is where prayer comes into play; talk to God the Father, and let Him know that you need Him, His protection, and His wisdom and guidance. God will even teach you how to deal with your spouse, communicate with your spouse, and relate with your spouse.

Let's take a look at the beginning, where everything took place. Everything started in the Garden of Eden. It was just Adam and

Eve; Adam was with Eve when she decided to grab a bite to eat, and while she went to grab fruit from the tree, there came the serpent. I want us to look at it to see that Adam and Eve were together; he ate the fruit Eve gave to him, so it was a physical separation that allowed the enemy to come in to talk to Eve's mind. So, the lesson is that husband and wife must be together in unity; whatever decisions they make must be together, but let us not be physically connected in disobedience with God. There was a time in my marriage when we were just newly married, and my husband moved immediately to New York. He was getting speaking engagements from left and right, and I had to work. At the time, I had to get up at 3:00 a.m. to be at work by 4:30 a.m., and I just felt like, at that time, why did I get married; I was alone; he was gone by the time I would get home, it would be short hours spent together. I began to cry out to the Lord and told the Lord how I felt. So one day, I came home from work, and my husband called me; he said baby, The Lord spoke to me today, and I had to pull over. I couldn't even drive, and he told me I needed to spend time with my wife. That's when I realized that if you do your part as a spouse, God will go before you and work out the kinks. 1 Peter 3:7 says, husbands, in the same way, be considerate as you live with your wives and treat them with respect as the weaker partner and as heirs with you of the gracious gift of life so that nothing will hinder your prayers.

#2 *stop telling people what's going on with you and your spouse*, especially those who do not have the spiritual foresight. You cannot tell everyone what your business is. Instead, you need to talk to God and seek out someone who has the spiritual insight to help you bring healing to your marriage.

#3 *If you want a change in your relationship, you must first be the product of change.* Always remember that it takes two and not one. There's always something that you can do better or change.

#4 *Always remember to convey your thoughts, feelings, and emotions under an even tone of voice*, and make sure that what you're saying is understood. Never assume anything.

#5 *Don't constantly complain because it will be perceived as nagging.* Remember, most people do not like to face their problems head-on; they run to the nearest exit.

#6 *Compromise..... compromise..... compromise.* We have to meet each other in the middle and agree.

Matthew 18 and 19 NIV say, again, I tell you that if two of you on earth agree about anything they ask for, it will be done for them by my Father in heaven.

Look at that power of agreement between two people; it can bring about change if you agree that the Father in heaven will honor your request.

Father, in the name of Jesus, I come before You on behalf of Your people today. Father, You have put together the unitary of marriage from the start in the Garden of Eden, which has continued till date, so I pray You to help us be united forever. We thank You, God, for the unity, and you, God, for the power of agreement that You put between two to be one. Thank You, God, because this is the institution You have ordained between a man and one who, I bind every hindrance that would come between, every trap of the Devil that will come to separate, that will come to draw apart two people that have been drawn together as one. I stand upon Your Word, which declares what God has joined together; let no man put asunder. God, at every difference between the two, I pray that You will give them the wisdom to come together and compromise to an agreement. We thank You, God, for the unity. We thank You for the many blessings that You have in store because Your Word says that when a man finds a wife, he obtains favor from You.

God, we give You glory, and we give You honor. Please, God, help the woman to honor her husband as the head of the household. May God be praised now that the man will learn to honor his wife. In the name of Jesus, we bind every witch, every warlock, and everything that has set out to destroy the two that have been joined together. Father, we declare today that no weapon formed against us shall prosper, and every lie that should rise against us in judgment shall be condemned. God, we will forever give Your name the praise, the glory, and the honor for now and always in Jesus' mighty name. Amen.

A daily prayer for you

Lord, help me to be a better wife or husband. Help me, God, use the tools You have put in me to bring us together.

CHAPTER 2: DEVELOPING A PRAYER A LIFE

Many say they pray daily, but I'm still in the same situation. When we pray, we look for a change in behavior, personal problems, finances, relationships, emotional healing, job status, help with children, etc.

The Lord showed me that we are praying with the intent that everything should change around us, but before change can occur in things that we prayed about, change must occur in us. We have to be the first product of change. One of the things I find is that people don't want to admit they are wrong. Please don't let self-righteousness fill your heart. There are always areas in our life that we can improve or change. I remember praying to God and asking Him to change some things in my home. My husband and I were in the storm, a financial storm. It seemed like every door we knocked on wouldn't open as you continue growing in the grace; God has to keep working His perfect work in you. Prayer has a way of fixing the insecurities or incompleteness in us. One thing that I changed was my language. I had to let go of negative words and speak positively and honestly.

Your perception

Have you ever had the feeling that you weren't fulfilling your purpose? What is the gift we have in us that we are supposed to develop or increase? What gift is supposed to bring us to the destination we are called to be in? We have two roads in life; one is what we want, and the second is what God wants. Which one do you think is more important? God's will! Some people find that purpose early in life, which is a blessing. What about those who don't find themselves until later on in adulthood? Most people show and associate the emptiness in their life with lowliness. Still, that is not an empty feeling in most cases if there is a feeling. Companionship can never fill the void that Jesus wants to complete in each of us. His Holy Spirit wants to see that eventually a prosperous fruit. Jesus Christ wants to be our everything, supplier, helper, protector, peace, joy, and even bread.

Matthew 6:33 says, seek his Kingdom and righteousness first, and all these things will also be given to you. I love that Scripture; that is my favorite Scripture even when I was a little girl. The Scripture tells us everything we need to get through life.

Seek the Lord first; that's what we do when we pray; we seek the Lord. We seek Him for answers, we seek Him for guidance, we seek Him for restoration, and we seek Him for help. All these things shall be added to us when we associate with God. Still, we usually associate that with worldly things. Before God enlarges all territory, He wants to enlarge His spirit within us. We know the earth is the Lord and everything that dwelleth therein. We know that cattle on 1000 Hills belonged to Him. We know that the Word declares that we shall ask anything in His name that He shall give it to us. But we forget the Scripture that says if we abide in Him, He will abide in us and that we should ask whatsoever we want, and He will give it to us. If we are honest with ourselves, are we giving 100% unto the Lord, or are we preserving 10% of ourselves and only giving 90 to the Lord? Or are we reserving 20% of ourselves and only giving God 80%? God wants a total surrender from us, and He doesn't want us to work in 10% of our power or 20% of our power; He wants us to rely upon Him with no reservation of thought due to our fleshly mentality.

CHAPTER 3:
BORN AGAIN

As we develop our prayer life, it brings about change. We are now what we call born again. When our mother conceived us, we were born in sin and shaped in iniquity.

So, we honor God our Father, and we recognize His deity. We recognize Him as being Holy. In the same way, we honor the judge when we go into the courtroom; they say all stand; the court is now in session to the honorable judge presiding.

Thy Kingdom is the spiritual ram over which God Reigns as King or the fulfillment on earth as God's will. God's ultimate purpose is to establish to Himself people a nation, a Kingdom. Peter establishes people. 1 Peter 2:9, But ye are a chosen generation, a royal priesthood, a holy nation, a peculiar people; that ye should shew forth the praises of him who hath called you out of darkness into his marvelous light; but ye are a chosen generation, a royal priesthood, a holy nation, a peculiar people; that ye should shew forth the praises of him who hath called. Verse 10 says, which in time past were not a people, but are now the people of God: which had not obtained mercy, but now have obtained mercy. God is looking for people that will be obedient to His Word.......Not to walk according to our feelings or our emotions. Most of the time, our feelings or emotions will lead us to a place of insecurity.

There are 12 and 9; let love be without dissimulation. Aboard that evil and cleave to that which is good. God has given us a set of laws to abide by to fulfill His Kingdom here on earth. God also wants us to work and forgive even as Christ forgave us.

Daily bread

The Lord is my Shepherd; I shall not want. This is what it means to give us Our Daily Bread. Bread is essential; we have to eat it to live. In the same way, we have to eat the Word of God for the Spirit of God to live within us and grow, which eventually will bring forth manifestation. This is also saying that He can give us what we need daily. Remember when the children of Israel were in the wilderness; they had just left Egypt and asked for food. Will God come down from heaven? They were only supposed to take the portion they would eat for that time on that day. Sometimes we want things we think we need, but it's unnecessary. Perhaps it is not in the will of God for our life at that particular time. Some things we ask are amiss because it's not the time or the season for what we want. It would be like giving a 5-year-old a car and saying, here are your keys; after that, put him under the wheel, and tell him to drive how maturity determines our possession. The children of Israel didn't make it into the Promised Land because they did not possess a level of maturity. Once God has revealed Himself and is evident in our lives, He is God. He's also expecting the spiritual part of man to mature over the flesh side of the man to walk in authority and confidence.

Forgiveness

God wants us to stay before Him in humility and not think of ourselves more highly than we ought to. As you continue your walk with the Lord, there will be some bumps and hindrances along the way. These things are a part of our growth which brings forth maturity. The children of Israel were at a place of forever learning and never able to come to the knowledge of the truth. This occurs when we're always making the same mistake, going around the same Mulberry tree, and growing through the same path. So we must continue as we pray to ask God for forgiveness. Forgiveness for the sins we are aware of and the sins we don't know of. Sometimes we omit what God tells us to do, which is a sin. He's also making us aware of the Scripture that if we want Him to forgive us, we must forgive those against us, those who have hurt us spitefully and used us, wrongfully accused us, and flat-out hate us without a cause. God wants us to be aware that we make mistakes too. This reminds me of a passage when the Pharisees and Sadducees came to Jesus with a question about a woman who was found in adultery; they asked Jesus what should be done with her. So Jesus stooped down and began to write, and He stood back up. He said he who is without sin cast the first stone. Jesus stood back down again and began to write, and when He came back up, He said to the woman where are the accusers? He told that woman to go her way and sin no more.

There was another passage about a servant who owed King some money, and the King went to him to collect the debt. And the man fell to his knees and began to ask for an extended time, and the King forgave him. That same servant had another man who owed him money, and the man fell next to the server for an extended time, but the servant didn't show the same compassion the King showed him. We must remember the mercy and pardon given to us and demonstrate love to someone else. We often categorize these types of sins as those we feel are more acceptable than others. I know, for example, we tend to show mercy to our children that when another person who's not blood-related falls short of the same sin, we tend to lower the hammer. Even so, we must show the same mercy to everyone.

CHAPTER 4:
UNSELFISH PRAYER

It is important to be conscious of the type of prayers we pray. Sometimes, we pray certain prayers in ignorance, not knowing what we're saying or asking God for. For instance, you must be very careful when asking God to help you be patient. When you pray like that, you should look for different challenges on your journey because you ask God to give you patience; He's developing your patience through different occurrences or His struggles with the storms of life.

Also, our thoughts, feelings, and hearts toward people. There was a man who was Caucasian and who was prejudiced, and he started to cause discord in our church. One day my cousin prophesied to him. She told him to cry out to God for more time. A couple of days later, we discovered he needed a triple bypass. I found myself asking why she prayed for him. All the trouble he was causing with all the hate in him. I realized I had to repent because he still deserved the chance to get right with God, even with all his evil. So, we are life speakers and believers. As the Scripture says, he that believes in him should have life and that more abundantly (John 3:16).

When some people pray, the only thing they think about is their family, their friends, and their loved ones. They don't think about anybody else who needs prayer. Pray for those on the street, pray for the ex-convict, pray for the drug addict, pray for the drug dealers, pray for the homosexuals, pray for the molesters, pray for the abuses of humanity. Pray for those rapists, pray for the murderers, pray for the children, pray for the countries, nationalities, and previous cities, pray for states, pray for leadership, the wealthy, pray for lawyers, pray for the judges, and pray for the police.

We need to pray for so many things and many people we need to stand in the gap for. You can start small and pray for your block; pray for a change in your street, whether a decent block or a drug-infested area. People must be saved, whether rich, black, white, or poor. There was a woman who prayed for a mountain to be moved, and she prayed every day for that mountain to be moved until one day, she woke up, and the heavy machinery was out there because the city officials wanted to make a railroad through the mountain. Remember that God will, and God can answer prayer.

Broken for the Master's use

There is a saying that it is hard to teach old dogs new tricks, which means when a person reaches a certain age of 30 and up, they're mostly set and the direction that is going in. Teenagers in their 20s are finding their way through life, making them more bendable and flexible. They're also more teachable than somebody who already knows or thinks they know.

When the Potter puts clay on the wheel, they spin it. At any point, Potter can decide that the product is not right; she squishes it all down to nothing and restarts to build the base again. So, the step to being made for God's use is #1 to acknowledge. #2 is submission.

Often, we ignore the true problem hindering us from moving forward because we don't want to go through the process of acknowledging it. If we acknowledge it, we stir up the pain that we have drowned deep inside us. Who wants to feel the hurt, and who wants to feel the pain so it is easier to act like it's never been there? Doing this causes us to not move forward, especially in God's things. One of the hindrances in my life was the fear of failure. I went to school to be a dialysis technician because I felt it was time to move on from being a nurse's assistant. One of the things that troubled me was that I had to put needles into people. I was troubled by the possibility that I would hurt someone. With the unknown that I might not be successful, it took a push from my mother and grandmother to apply for a job hiring dialysis technicians. I lost about 20 pounds in the first month of my training. I'm glad that I went through this process. Today, I wouldn't have a testimony to know that God will see you through and strengthen you to complete the task. We are our own biggest hindrance.

One of the things we struggle with is the fear of the unknown. Faith is easy when you can see it! It is easy when you can see the path you're going in, but when we walk in unknown territory, there is always the fear of what if......... This is where submission comes in. God wants a total yes of giving over to His will, power, and authority. When we release, we give everything to Him; that is when we see faith walking. God does not tell us everything; He tells us things as we go; that's the whole point of trust. Trust in the Lord with all your heart. When you have the Savior by your side, you don't have to be afraid of going through the process; He will be with you, never leave you, and not forsake you. I trusted Him by letting go and believing Him to see me through. I worked as a Dialysis tech for over ten years. Yes, I did it through Jesus Christ, who strengthened me.

One year, I went to Jamaica, and there was a place called Dunns River Falls, and we climbed up the fall with the help of a team of workers. I said to myself; I want to conquer my fear of Heights. I am afraid of Heights... So, after the assistants left, my cousin and I decided that we were going to climb the fall by ourselves. I was at a point where the water was beating in my face, and I felt like I couldn't take another step. I was holding on for dear life and saying; this is it; I'm going to die. A stranger came out of nowhere and helped me up that Cliff. It was then that I realized it is not the physical fear of things we need to overcome but things that prevent us from progressing.

Let's talk about what causes us to be afraid: Different adult fluencies, maybe family history, stop pier associations that bring about peer pressure, maybe it was a personal encounter, or maybe low self-esteem. I want you to know that God is a healer of more than just the physical body elements. He is a Healer of the mind and the soul.

It was back in 1992 when I started playing the organ for my dad. I heard so many stories about how people were prayed for, and automatically they just started playing the piano or the organ. I said I wanted that same experience because I didn't want to put in the hard work it took to be a great player. I felt bad then that music didn't come to me naturally as others. And I thought that God should give it to me, but He didn't. Also, I was not thankful and didn't see when God was increasing my playing, even though I didn't take the time to practice. I hated practicing. I wanted to sound just like those professionals, and I didn't have that sound when I practiced. People tell me that they enjoyed my playing, and I would look at them like they were crazy, like stop, you're lying. A couple of years down the road, I decided that I would give up. I would play until they found another organist, but until then, I had given up in my heart, and in my mind, I was done. That Sunday, after church, I went outside and said hello to my cousin; she was on her way to her car, then she doubled back, and she said the Lord said I don't give it up, but it was too late. I had already committed in my heart that I was done. It wasn't until later that I realized what God was trying to teach me.

Everything in life doesn't come easy, nor is it handed to you with a golden spoon. You have to work at it, and then God will give the increase. When you seek God, you don't seek God on Sunday and then don't return to Him on Monday. It is a constant seeking God daily. In your endurance and persistence in yielding to His will, He steps in and delivers. I didn't realize how much I had a passion for playing. I pushed it away deep down inside of me, trying to erase it from my mind until 2017 when God told me to go back to school for music. God blew my mind because I didn't know He thought that much of me to give me another chance to do what I am supposed to do. The Scriptures say, "the thoughts I have of you are peace and not evil to bring you to your expected end." (Jer 29:11)

If you are wondering why you are still going through the same situation or still going around that same Mulberry Bush, you're not submitting to the process. You must remember that to become a diamond, you must be put under pressure. If you have emptiness, God will fill that void. He will give you your heart's desire according to His will for your life.

I never saw myself as prideful, yet I had a lot of pride in me that I had never recognized before; it was only when my husband and I were in a financial storm that it became a turning point in my life. In that time of testing, I began to seek God like never before. And He became more real in my life than ever. The spirit of God is not going to go over your will. God is not a controlling God; that's not his character. During this testing time, I realized I had to let pride go. Sometimes God uses the same people that have talked about you and put you down to bless you. You could spend a lifetime proving to people that you're blessed or prosperous. I realize that you can't please people but can please God. So pride had to go. The Scripture says, "He will make your enemies your footstool." I have heard some say that God will cause you to step on your enemies, but in all reality, it is that your enemies will not triumph over you. To be a true servant of God, you must be pride-free. Remember that the meek shall inherit the earth.

CHAPTER 5:
PATIENCE

Through my experiences, I've learned that you can't hurry God; you must wait. I know we live in an age where everything is fast. We have a microwave we use to warm the food up quickly. We have a fast-paced lifestyle; now, we have vacuum cleaners that move independently and the Alexa LEXIS equipment. We could speak to Alexis and tell Alexis what to do, and it would happen. The new technology is here to save time.

Sometimes we get so caught up with time stipulations that we put expectations and time limits on where we should be. We have a vision board with a 10-year goal: get married in two years, have a baby in three years, buy a house, and, not to forget, climb up the corporate ladder. We forget that God is the Father of time. I tried to remind myself that one day with the Lord is as 1000 years and 1000 years as one day. The Father doesn't want to give us desires we are not ready for. But He's a type of God who wants to prepare us for the gifts He gives us. My husband often tells the story of how he wanted to get his elder license, and his pastor at the time felt that he was not ready, and he said to him, "boy giving you an elder license is like putting a shotgun to your head." Just because we plan for certain things to occur at a certain time doesn't always mean they will happen at the expected time. Don't be discouraged! Remember, man has time limits, but there are no time limitations with God. He can cause the impossible to be possible.

James 1:4-8 King James Version (KJV)

4 But let patience have her perfect work, that ye may be perfect and entire, wanting nothing.

We have to stay the course, for God knows the way we should take. There was a time when I gave myself five years of going through financial hardship based on the events in the Bible and how long it took them to be free from their situation. So, five years came, and I said, Lord, when will You deliver me? Let my enemy see me being exalted. You discover what people think of you when you go through difficult times, trials, and storms. As they did Job, Job's friends called him a goody-two-shoes; you must have done something wrong to go through this Calamity. And so, when my five years came, I was still going through it. God didn't come and deliver me, and my faith was sure that God would deliver me. I fell into such a depression. I said what am I here for? What is my purpose? What am I doing? What am I doing wrong? What is it I'm not doing right? The Lord used my Godfather to pray for me out of my depression. I have learned that there is no TIME in God. There is no expected time limit. One thing you can bank on is that God wants to complete us and make us perfect! Go through the process, giving God the praise, knowing that he is our hope and he never fails. It is important to remember the promises of God; write them down in your notebook or your Journal, so you can go back to them later and look at them when you are feeling a little down. One thing about it is that God is not slack concerning His promises; He is faithful and just.

So, remember that everything is not in our time expectancy; it is always in His timing. You cannot predict you're coming out of the season and can't prophesy your way out. There are just some things you must go through; everybody has a wilderness experience to walk through.

The things I learned in my wilderness experience are:

---

1) To be the wife God has called me to be, I had to change. There is a saying," you can draw more bees with honey." Love conquerors all.

2) It is not the expectations of others toward me but how I see myself.

3) Hearing the voice of God is important. Remember, every word is established out of the mouth of 2 or 3 witnesses. Not to lean in my understanding but in everything to acknowledge Jesus.

4) To wait on God for an answer!

5) Stop complaining, and start thanking. I think it is imperative to ask God to give you a prayer partner who can pray with you and to whom you can talk. This person is someone that is not going to hold things against you. This person is not going to spread your business everywhere. This person is going to pray and leave at the altar literally. This person will not give you their opinion but will give wise advice.

Let us also consider how long it took for Abraham and Sarah to receive the promise. God promised Abraham and Sarah a child, and they waited 25 years. When God makes a promise to us, we often think automatically, OK, tomorrow it's coming, or it will be here by next week, or we're going to give it three months down the road, and it's coming. Sarah had to wait 25 years. She got anxious between waiting and told Abraham to go and be with her maid. Just like us, we sometimes get anxious, and we try to figure things out independently on our own. How am I going to make this come to pass? We must remember that God partly gives us things, so we don't see the full picture. I think the hardest thing is trying to figure out how God will make this happen, the exploitation of the unknown. We, the human race, must be in control, knowing the start and finish of everything. The hardest part of faith is dealing with the unknown, but God wants our full reliance upon Him, so patience is part of letting go and letting God be God. (See Genesis 12: 15-17).

In everything, there is an appointed time. I don't think you should pray for patience or ask God to give you patience. The best thing is to start to identify when you feel anxious. It might be when you are presented with an idea or business plan, and without reservations, you move on to another person's word. It is wise to gather as much information as possible. Get an idea of where you are going and what to expect. Then, the next step is to go to the Father in prayer. Ask God to show you. Take a deep breath and count down from ten, and release. This is just one suggestion to help slow down and process your thoughts until we align with God's word. Let us get out of the habit of telling God what to do and get into the practice of asking Him.

When I was younger, I believe I was still in elementary school. One day, I asked my dad if I could go to the roller rink with a friend, and I believe it took him about half an hour to answer.

Certain jobs can help build your patience. If you do any direct care with people in the healthcare field, it will teach you patience. Even in the grocery store, the customer is always right according to the rule. So, believe it or not, having patience is all around us ......we pick and choose what we will have patience with. Patience and waiting on the Lord will keep us from making wrong decisions.

I think the reason for so many divorces in this country is that people don't want to wait.

Yes, there is no patience. Marriage requires patience. In today's world, as soon as a problem arises, the spouse is ready to leave the marriage. The quote is: "I can do all bad by myself."

The Scripture says, but they that wait upon the Lord shall renew their strength; they shall mount up with wings as eagles... (Isaiah 40:31)

Remember that even when you're feeling at your lowest and you can't take it anymore.

God promises to restore your strength so you can make it another day.

CHAPTER 6:
2 CHRONICLES 7:14

"if my people, who are called by my name, will humble themselves and pray and seek my face and turn from their wicked ways, then I will hear from heaven, and I will forgive their sin and will heal their land." NIV.

This Scripture is often quoted in different church settings, and its meaning dissipates because of its frequent use. Even God's name has gotten frequent usage until it becomes like any other name. We have been told down through the years that Jesus is coming back again until the people have stopped believing. The reason for this is the misunderstanding of this Scripture or verse. When we hear that Jesus is soon to come, we think of that Great Day when Jesus cracks the sky, but in reality, it is when Jesus calls your name to leave this earth and when Jesus cracks the sky.

DEFINITION OF "IF" (introducing a conditional clause) on the condition or supposition that; if something should occur that the people are not compliant, I have a solution for you. Let's give thanks to His grace and mercy. God is so awesome that He knew beforehand that we would mess up, so He gave us an escape. Anytime you fall into a situation, even with your stubbornness, the Lord Jesus makes a way to escape for us. We don't have an excuse because He has given us a way out.

The question is, what is hindering us from obtaining the promise? We serve a God that supplies all we need according to His riches and glory.

Rev 12:10. …Now is come Salvation strength, and the Kingdom of our God and the power of his Christ…

Often, He suffers from stumbling blocks because we don't keep in remembrance of our Christian history. You know of the children of Israel and the laws and statutes given to them by Moses. Those ceremonies and memorials are part of our learning. Located in the Old Testament is the feast of the tabernacles. This holiday is also known as **Sukkot**. This reminded the Jews of how God protected them in their 40-year exodus from Egypt to the Promised Land.

The feast of the Passover was to commemorate the liberation of the rule of Israel, who was led out of Egypt by Moses.

We must remember the things God has done, both past and present. Satan comes to rob, steal, and destroy. Well, what does he come to steal? He comes to take out joy and make us forget the goodness of Jesus in our lives. That is a slow process, and history has shown that it is very effective. Through time, love for God slowly dissipates into an image of him being just a man. You have to remember that only moments in the Garden of Eden that Eve has another outlook on what God had said. Just that quickly, our perception of who God is changed. The key point is, what shall separate us from the love of God? How can people who have seen the powers of the true and living God and had seen and witnessed His miracles forget the gracious power of His love? God is so omnipotent that He knew there would be a great chance that His people would mess up, that He said I would leave an avenue or path so that when they lose their way, they can find me again.

IF MY PEOPLE WHO ARE CALLED BY MY NAME.....

Older people are those that have heard the knocking at the door and have answered the call. The Scripture says, "Behold I stand at the door knocking if you hear my voice and open the door, I will come in, to him and eat with him, and he with me." (Rev 3:20)

God is only calling sinners to repentance. He is calling His people to be saints and to follow the example of Christ. In the Garden of Eden, after they had eaten the fruit, God said to Adam, "Where are you?"

If We Humble Ourselves

How do we humble ourselves before the throne of grace? We have to come before Him in the likeness of a child. The Scripture reference is: (Luke 18:16).

But Jesus called them unto him, and said, suffer little children to come unto me, and forbid them not: for of such is the Kingdom of God.

Children are innocent, vulnerable, and sensitive to their parent's voices; they seek to please their parents, and when a child receives correction, they are sorrowful.

I remember being a young child, about nine years of age, and I could remember knowing when my mother was sad or happy. I was sensitive to knowing what mood she was in. I was sensitive to her tone of voice.

So, we have to acknowledge God as being Abba (Father). The one we depend on and lean on. So, He is the Daddy, and we are the children. Sometimes as adults, we don't take full ownership of our mistakes. Like in the Garden of Eden, Eve passed the blame to the serpent, and Adam passed the blame to the woman. We need to take ownership of our mistakes. When we come to God the Father, we must acknowledge His authority and be open to what He says. For they that worship him must worship in spirit and truth. (John 4:24)

He knows everything about us and is waiting for us to come to Him. Jesus wants us to come unto Him and learn of Him. Jesus is Our Very Present Help. We pray to God for everything we need, home, car, and family, but we forget to ask Him to forgive our sins of what we know and don't know. The Lord Jesus paid the price so that we could be renewed, changed, and transformed into the image of Christ. It is His will for us to be better individuals at whatever we do or are called. We shouldn't strive for masteries of the things of this world well; we should strive for a closer connection with the Lord Jesus, our supplier.

Turn from our wicked ways

Although we ask God to forgive us since we never change our behavior patterns, it might be that we're not aware of what our sins are. If you pray, Lord, bring your sins before me; he will answer and show you what your sins are. There have been times I have prayed to the Lord to show me what You don't like about me, and He answered. I remember the Lord showed me that I was eating in places that offered their food to idols. I told the Lord that I wouldn't eat in another ungodly restaurant. This place was not fit for His people to dine in there. We must be careful of what we watch, the places we go, and even our garments. I have learned to question everything brought before me because I want to know who made it and for what purpose. Everything about us has to be changed over unto His will. So we pray, Lord, may Your will be done in me for God's will to be done on earth; we have to be the first partakers of change to bring about change on earth.

CHAPTER 7:
HEAR FROM HEAVEN

Anytime there was any affliction or destruction to that ruler, Israel, there was a separation between them and God. If your phone line with someone and static is present, eventually you will lose connection. The static was keeping us from hearing God and from God hearing us. The static represents sin! Once the connection is restored, we can hear clearly. So God is saying He will hear us and remove the destruction and the pollution in the land. The land will become fruitful and prosperous. Once we are restored, we will have Dominion. He will give us the land we did not toil on and houses we did not build. So, we have to get in position and gain our authority back. We have to get into a place where we can hear God, and He can hear us.

Prayer warrior

I think many questions arise when it comes to intercessory prayer. Well, let's talk about intercessory. What is an intercessor? A dictionary definition is someone who intervenes on behalf of another, especially by prayer. A warrior is a person that fights a battle. The dictionary definition is (especially in former times) a brave or experienced soldier or fighter.

A warrior is a person that is strong in the Lord. The United States army puts you through different tests to ensure that the person has what it takes to be in the army. You also have to be able to follow orders when given. Guess what? Sometimes, your commanding officers are not nice. Is everyone a prayer warrior? The answer is no. You must be called to that office like any other gift or position. I thank God for the gifts of the body because it is for the improvement of the church.

Jer. 9:17-18

Thus, saith the LORD of hosts, consider ye, and call for the mourning women, that they may come; and send for cunning women, that they may come:

Every church should have prayer warriors interceding for the ministry and its leaders. Warriors stand in the gap, just as Jesus is now waiting for us before His Father.

Prayer warriors are not just praying for people because the Scripture says that men should always pray and not faint. You labor before the Lord in the spirit when you are a warrior. The Holy Ghost takes you into the secret things. The Holy Ghost will have you praying for different people, not knowing their situations, but you will cry out for them. When you are a warrior, the church's concern is at your heart to the point that it hurts to see the low condition of the body of Christ. Let's look at Mary and Martha on how they were concerned about Jesus' body. They couldn't sleep; they were concerned about their Lord's body until the angel had to meet them at the tomb. Sometimes, the warriors can lead the church into the spirit of crying out before God and learning how to wait on Him to respond. Remember that the Lord hears and delivers the cry of the righteous. Sometimes when I pray, the Lord takes me into a cry, so sometimes, I can't pray a short prayer. After I finish praying, the Lord often takes me into praise of a dance. He will lead you into praise before the battle is over!

Please use this section to journal what the Holy Spirit is revealing to you.

www.ingramcontent.com/pod-product-compliance
Lightning Source LLC
Chambersburg PA
CBHW070321120526
44590CB00017B/2766